I0814401

DISCOVER ANCIENT CIVILIZATIONS

Ancient Greece

by M.J. York

CAPSTONE VALUE LIBRARY
a capstone imprint

Published by Capstone® Value Library, an imprint of Capstone
1710 Roe Crest Drive, North Mankato, Minnesota 56003
capstonepub.com

Library of Congress Cataloging-in-Publication Data is available on the Library of Congress website
ISBN: 9798875306754 (hardcover)
ISBN: 9798875306785 (ebook PDF)

Summary: An exploration of the history and legacy of ancient Greece.

Editorial Credits
Editor: Kellie M. Hultgren; Designer: Jennifer Walker; Production Specialist: Tori Abraham

Image Credits
Dreamstime: Anyaivanova, 23, Charalambos Andronos, 13, Fritz Hiersche, 9, Scaliger, 21, Sergey Novikov, 7; Getty Images: Nick Brundle Photography, cover; Shutterstock: Achim Wagner, 17, DaLiu, 5

Printed and bound in the USA. 006585

Table of Contents

CHAPTER 1

Ancient Greece

The ancient Greeks were a seafaring people. They lived on the islands and **peninsulas** where the modern country of Greece is today. By the 700s BCE, the ancient Greeks had their own writing and culture. The people built many cities. Sometimes the cities were allies, and sometimes they fought.

Many ancient Greek ideas are still important. The Greeks had the first **democracy** where the people voted on their leaders. Greeks wrote the first histories. Modern math and science owe many ideas to the Greeks. Greek legends and myths are told and retold even today.

The Acropolis of Lindos stands on one of the many islands in the Aegean Sea where ancient Greeks lived.

CHAPTER 2

Mountains and Seas

Greece has many mountains. The people lived on many small islands too. Travel was difficult in ancient times. It was easier by sea than by land.

Because of the geography, each Greek city ruled itself. The farmlands near it provided food. The city and the lands around it were called a **city-state**. Most city-states were small. Athens and Sparta were the largest.

Greek ships crisscrossed the Mediterranean Sea. Their crews traded for goods and created **colonies**. They wanted land for farming and good harbors for their ships.

The ruins of the stadium in Delphi remain on the steep slopes of Mount Parnassus.

CHAPTER 3

Greek Democracy

Democracy began in ancient Greece. Each city-state had its own leaders. In early centuries, chiefs or groups of wealthy men ruled. In the 600s BCE, **citizens** of Sparta elected a council to rule. However, only Spartan soldiers could be citizens.

Beginning in the 500s BCE, citizens of Athens met together to make decisions for the city. The city's many tribes also elected a council that ran the government. Men born in Athens who were not enslaved were citizens. But across Greece, many people were enslaved. Many peasant farmers were not citizens either.

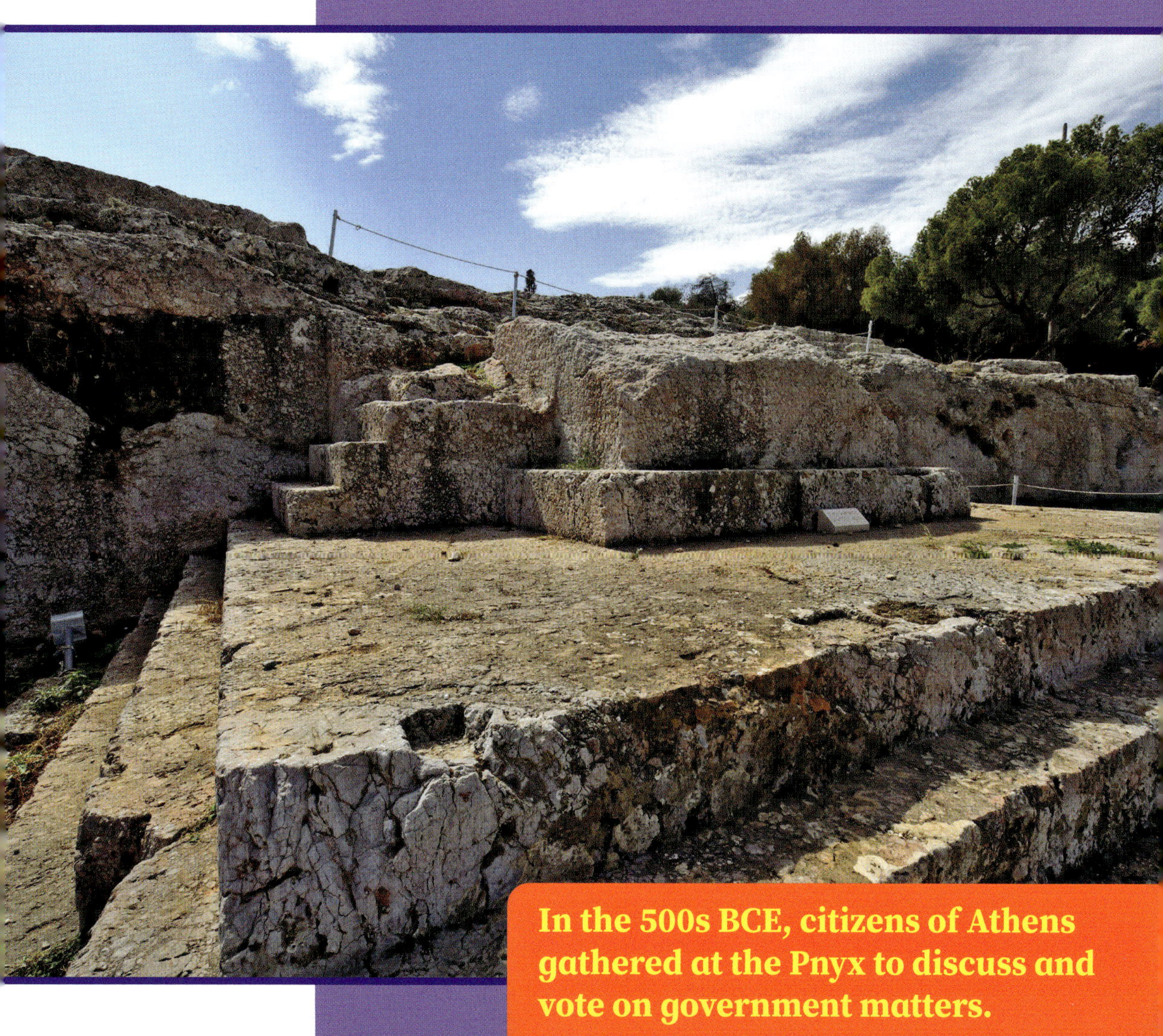

In the 500s BCE, citizens of Athens gathered at the Pnyx to discuss and vote on government matters.

War and Empire

The city-states went to war often. However when the Persian Empire attacked in the 400s BCE, the city-states fought together. Decades later, Athens expanded its borders. Athens and Sparta battled many times.

In 336 BCE, Alexander the Great rose to power. He was from a Greek region called Macedon. He was only 20 years old. Swiftly he conquered Greece, Egypt, Persia, and the rest of the Middle East. His empire reached from Europe to India. He founded cities and brought trade. He never lost a battle. But after only 13 years as king, he died in 323 BCE. His empire fell apart. It was the end of the ancient Greek era.

CHAPTER 4

Home Life

Most Greeks were farmers. They raised sheep and goats. They grew barley, wheat, olives, grapes, and figs. On the coast they fished.

Most homes were made of mud bricks, plaster, and wood. Some had two stories. Rooms opened around a courtyard. Houses usually shared walls with their neighbors.

Women spun wool and made cloth. Men and women wore large pieces of cloth draped and pinned at the shoulder. They wore cloaks and tunics, too.

A carving from a cemetery in Athens shows two men and a woman wearing draped clothing.

Men who were citizens needed a good education. They studied math and economics. They learned to be good public speakers. Boys went to school and learned from mentors. They learned fitness, music, and literature. Girls learned stories, songs, and weaving at home. Women could not be citizens. They had few rights.

Food and Fitness

Ancient Greeks ate a lot of porridge and bread. They ate lentils and vegetables but little meat. They liked fish fresh, pickled, and dried.

Being strong was important for Greek warriors. In Sparta, boys left home at age 7. They were raised together to be soldiers. Greek men worked out in the city's gymnasium. This space was often a school too. Some women also exercised.

Beginning in 776 BCE, Greeks came together every four years for the Olympic games. The first recorded games just had a footrace. More events were added later. Men raced and wrestled. They threw the **discus** and the **javelin**. Winners were crowned with a wreath of olive leaves. Women ran a separate race.

CHAPTER 5

Art and Science

We know a lot about the Greeks from their art. They carved elegant statues from white marble and painted them in bright colors. Many vases show gods and goddesses, legends, and scenes from daily life.

We still read Greek **tragedies**, **comedies**, and poems. Two Greek epic poems are the *Iliad* and the *Odyssey*. They tell about heroes and gods in an ancient war. People still read these stories today and connect with their themes and characters.

Socrates, Plato, and Aristotle are famous **philosophers** from Athens. They thought about the law and society. They wondered what it means to be good. They wanted to understand truth and the meaning of life. We still debate their ideas today.

A painted vase shows the warriors Achilles and Ajax playing a board game as the goddess Athena watches.

Science and Military

The Greeks used math, logic, and observation to study the world. This is the beginning of modern science. They built clocks and experimented with levers and gears. **Astronomers** watched the stars and learned about eclipses. Greek doctors carefully examined patients so their medical skills improved. Greeks studied numbers and geometry. They learned that Earth is a round sphere that spins and they discovered how large it is.

Greek armies had some of the best technology of the time. The trireme ship had three decks. It needed 170 rowers. The Greek soldier was called a hoplite. He had armor, a helmet and shield, and a spear or sword. Soldiers fought in a tight group called a phalanx. There were also cavalry troops on horses.

CHAPTER 6

Gods and Goddesses

The Greeks prayed to many gods and goddesses. They built beautiful temples with tall columns. They held festivals and **rituals** to honor the gods.

Each region had its own gods. But over time some became the most widely worshipped. The Greeks prayed to the goddess Aphrodite for luck in love. They prayed to Athena for wisdom and courage. Poseidon was god of the sea, and Ares was god of war. Zeus was king of the gods and weather. He could protect or punish.

Greeks told many stories about their gods. The gods acted very human. They could be kind or cruel. The stories helped people understand their world. They helped people lead good lives.

This bronze statue once held a weapon and may show the god Zeus.

CHAPTER 7

The Legacy of Greece

Greek art and architecture inspired the Roman civilization that came after. They also inspired the Renaissance in Europe in the 1500s CE. Many buildings today still have Greek-style columns.

Today, the Parthenon built by the Ancient Greeks remains. It is a temple to Athena. Its tall columns still awe visitors. We study ruins of temples, theaters, and buildings across the Greek world.

The Greeks wanted to be remembered. They built to last. They invented written history. Their poems, plays, and stories are the basis of modern European literature. When we listen, we can still hear their voices today.

The Parthenon was built during the 400s BCE.

Glossary

astronomers (uh-STRAH-nuh-muhrz)—people who study stars and the night sky

citizens (SI-tuh-zuhnz)—members of a state or people who can participate in a government

city-state (SI-tee-STAYT)—region that consists of a city and its surrounding lands that govern themselves

colonies (KAH-luh-neez)—areas over which a distant country or people hold control

comedies (KAH-muh-deez)—Ancient Greek plays that include humor and a happy ending

democracy (di-MAH-kruh-see)—form of government where the people have power to make laws and elect representatives

discus (DISS-kuhss)—heavy disc made of stone or metal

javelin (JAV-uh-luhn)—light spear that is thrown for distance

peninsulas (puh-NIN-suh-luhz)—portions of land mostly surrounded by water

philosophers (fuh-LOSS-uh-furz)—people who seek wisdom and understanding

rituals (RICH-oo-uhlz)—established forms, actions, or words of a ceremony

tragedies (TRAJ-uh-deez)—Ancient Greek plays about right and wrong, often religious, with a sad ending

Index